Baby Farm Animals

Baby Goats

By Nick Rebman

level 1
little blue readers

www.littlebluehousebooks.com

Copyright © 2022 by Little Blue House, Mendota Heights, MN 55120. All rights reserved. No part of this book may be reproduced or utilized in any form or by any means without written permission from the publisher.

Little Blue House is distributed by North Star Editions:
sales@northstareditions.com | 888-417-0195

Produced for Little Blue House by Red Line Editorial.

Photographs ©: Shutterstock Images, cover, 4, 7, 9, 11, 12–13, 14, 17, 19, 20, 22–23, 24 (top left), 24 (top right), 24 (bottom left), 24 (bottom right)

Library of Congress Control Number: 2021916723

ISBN
978-1-64619-475-9 (hardcover)
978-1-64619-502-2 (paperback)
978-1-64619-555-8 (ebook pdf)
978-1-64619-529-9 (hosted ebook)

Printed in the United States of America
Mankato, MN
012022

About the Author

Nick Rebman is a writer and editor who lives in Minnesota. He enjoys reading, drawing, and taking long walks with his dog.

Table of Contents

Learning to Walk **5**

Eating and Drinking **15**

Playing and Growing **21**

Glossary **24**

Index **24**

Learning to Walk

I see a baby goat.

It is wet when it is born.

I see a baby goat.

The mother licks it clean.

I see a baby goat.

It stands up.

I see a baby goat.

Soon it can walk.

I see a baby goat.

It sleeps near its mother.

Eating and Drinking

I see a baby goat.

It gets milk from its mother.

I see a baby goat.

It drinks water from a tub.

I see a baby goat.

It starts to eat plants.

Playing and Growing

I see a baby goat.

It plays with another goat.

I see a baby goat.

It starts to grow horns.

Glossary

horns

plants

milk

water

Index

M
mother, 6, 12, 15

P
play, 21

S
sleep, 12

T
tub, 16